A HOUSE REJOICING

❖ ❖ ❖

Poems by Pavel Chichikov

GREY OWL PRESS

Pavel Chichikov is a Washington, DC–based poet and photographer. He has written for both the secular and the Catholic press on issues as diverse as Russian nuclear weapons systems, Olympic athletes, and miracles. His books include *Lion Sun: Poems by Pavel Chichikov* (Grey Owl Press, 1999), *Miracles and Stations in the Manner of Ignatius* (Kaufmann Publishing, 2005), *Animal Kingdom* (Kaufmann Publishing, 2009), and *From Here to Babylon* (Grey Owl Press, 2010). Pavel may be heard reading his works on catholicradiointernational.com. His poetry regularly appears on "The Poetry of Pavel Chichikov," pavelspoetry.com.

© 2012 by Pavel Chichikov

Grey Owl Press
1211 Holly Street NW, Washington DC 20012
http://pavelspoetry.com

Printed in the United States of America
Cover image: "The Little Festive House," Lisa Lorenz Paintings©

ISBN: 0967190185
ISBN-13: 9780967190181
Library of Congress Control Number: 2012943177
CreateSpace, North Charleston, SC
∞ *Printed on acid-free paper*

CONTENTS

For Jonathan,
in courage and spirit

A HOUSE REJOICING

Enter here, there is July
An arch of laurel overhead,
Here is a room of ivory,
Moonlight on the fields for bed

You may sleep or you may wake
To walk the corridors of this
Mansion, any way you take
Will lead to love, no one can miss

Servants padding silently
To serve the ones who enter thus
Have larger eyes with which to see,
They will not wake the sleeping guests

Some have wings and some have feet
And some have both with which they go
To snuff the candles, are discreet
Because they know what is to know

That all have come from darkness here,
This is a special form of night
In which there is no dark to fear,
A house rejoicing being bright

❧ ❧ ❧

2 KINGS 2:6–14

Elijah slapped his mantle down, the river parted,
When they crossed it was not to the other side
But to some other place, outside of time—
The chasm between here and there is wide

Down came the chariot, crimson flame and ardor,
Burning horses, flashing reins and thunder,
This apparition of another place, triumphant power—
It was the world of common sense that tore asunder

We too then will cross, for when the river separates
We will cross over to another place; deliver us,
Come meet us when the flowing river parts—
Even now the currents that obstruct are tremulous

❖ ❖ ❖

AN ACT OF PEACE

During Mass, a church in France—
The Wehrmacht occupied the town—
A congregant whose near relations
Were all inside—the town was small—
Left for need, for nature's summons,
Gained the street, he saw at once
A German soldier, grim, immense
Who hissed to him: "Like to survive?
Yes? Then beat it, stay alive"
The church was cordoned, blessings cursed,
Special Forces and much worse
Braced for action, bent on vengeance
For killings by the French Resistance

Away, away, those Catholics called
To meet their doom at Buchenwald
While he, the youth, the sole survivor
Became of doom the countersigner,
One set free if others died
As though, the grace of God denied,
A witness made as if to be
Of senseless death the notary

Then the soldier who released
The witness who was not a priest
Nor pious yet could testify
To how by chance they came to die
Who wished to be at Mass that day,
Were picked out randomly to slay
Because they gathered in one place—
One putsch and half the town erased

But why the mercy of that man,
Why that time and place to stand?
What purpose and what reason for
An act of peace and not of war?

❖ ❖ ❖

Pavel Chichikov

IT WILL NOT THRIVE

At last the state intolerant
Will find a way to track them down,
Those anarchists, those malcontents
By chip and GPS and drone

Because it cannot tolerate
Disorder in the uniform
Imperative that is the state,
The future canon they deform

Although they drivel sabotage,
Disruption of the ways and means,
None of them can stay at large
Because they are both heard and seen

Some will be retained and turned
To hunt the others, bait and switch
So that the one the other burns,
Fanatic by fanatic snitch

Useless, helpless violent dreams
Destroying what they terminate,
A recapitulating scheme,
Decentralized surveillance states

Age or perish, they go by
As other cadres take their place,
Soon there will be no more "I"
But only we who have no face

Who can stop the progress of
Secretion of the human hive,
Human power lacking love
Will die of grief, it will not thrive

❖ ❖ ❖

DEMONS WHO AGREE

The simple summon power
To scatter all deceit,
Confound the wrong with terror,
Set justice on her feet

But they will be wrong-footed
By demons who agree
That evil is deep rooted
And greed an ancient tree

Here, receive the broadax,
Grasp the maul and wedge,
Use the pit and saw
To slice up privilege

But when they stand in dust
That tree will still be tall,
For power grows from power
And rises from its fall

❖ ❖ ❖

WHAT POWER IN US?

She has obstructive lung disease,
The worse it is the less she breathes,
Though her dosage will increase
The anguish of it will not cease

Another med can give remoteness,
Severance from pain and horror,
Strangled by her own dead lungs
She will not at this stage recover

She wants to know if she can skip
This stage of dying, must it be
That slowly from us we are ripped,
Can we not at once go free?

Come at once, come at once
You angels and you messengers;
But no they seem not to advance
Beyond these pangs, those harbingers

What dreadful lesson do You teach,
What regimen of self-denial?
Have mercy on us we beseech,
What punishment is this, what trial?

What power in us to atone?
The sun is conquered overhead,
Christ will vanquish death alone,
About the city walk the dead

❧ ❧ ❧

Pavel Chichikov

COMFORT PACK

They've ordered her a comfort pack
As if by dying she would lack
Relief from agony alone
To roll away the heavy stone

That bulks across the tomb of life
As if morphine were death's midwife;
There is something more to come,
None will enter except one

We have never seen that room
The private sanctum of that tomb,
Nor will we enter except once
Alone to see what she confronts

What figure, court, what light and shade
That is for all not long delayed,
What joy of grain, what flower-wheat,
What premonition life defeats

What glory and what company,
What gate descending will she see?
Which flowers and what rising stair,
What sense to hear the harp of air

Like music flowing over leaves,
What colors weaving through the trees
Like ribbons of supernal silk,
What carp of gold, what streams like milk?

And then the meeting of a kind
That will not fit within the mind
So large a figure will there be,
Though face to face with you and me

There is no room within that pack
For love that will make up its lack,
As small as many, great as may
Give comfort on the last first day

❖ ❖ ❖

Pavel Chichikov

ONE I KNEW…

One I knew
Cursed death
As if it were a figure in a hood
A skeleton and scythe
A visitor, a revenant
A walker in the night

The death you curse is death in you
It wears your face
It breathes the sour breath of rage
And at the banquet of rejoicing
Takes your place,
Spills the wine
Tramples on the bread,
It is the death in you
And in it you become the dead

To cast it out?
Evict what is the root of death in you?
Curse it not
Not even death
Curse nothing that is true
And it will leave
When death has had the time to grieve

❖ ❖ ❖

BLESS THE CHILD

Swinging on a Mulberry
The bough is weak, the child comes down,
And though she cries incessantly
The hurt is lesser than the sound

Deer that fatten in the wood
Lick up the berries and get high,
The fruit fermented, sugared, stewed
In violent sunshine and the sky

Birds commanding energy
To feed and satisfy their brood
Peck the berries happily,
A little high, a little stewed

And there are worms who also feed
On mulberry but just the leaves,
An emperor of China needs
A silken robe with silken sleeves

The Mulberry is generous,
The birds, the deer, the emperor
Receive the crop and it will bless
The child and will not trouble her

❖ ❖ ❖

Pavel Chichikov

MY HEART

They led me to the frail sick foal,
The head hung flaccid on the sill,
Children told me I must heal it
As if they knew I could restore it

Emaciated, almost black
How can my pity bring it back?
What is the helpless foal, its eyes
Are great moist wounds without surprise

If I can touch it will it heal?
What cure the pity that I feel?
Will it flourish, will I ride?
Is it the soul of me inside?

First you will restore the heart—
But with what treatment shall I start?
Only see what I have done
To lead you here, my heart, my son

❖ ❖ ❖

VIRGIN MILK

On a train through Spanish country
Spanish women start to sing,
Smile their praises of the Virgin,
Offerings of laughter ring

One refrain goes to another,
They clap their hands to spread the rhythm,
The whole car full and yet together,
Happiness and peace to hymn

They praise the warmth of motherhood
Which nothing sullies or destroys,
The virgin milk of wonderment
With which she fed the baby boy

❖ ❖ ❖

THE ENTERTAINER

I saw human suffering
Who danced a funny step,
Loose-limbed, slow and casual,
Angular, adept

An entertainer not a clown,
He had a pleasant smile,
Astonishing to see him so—
I watched him for a while

He danced inside a shopping mall
As shoppers passed him by,
Very thin and very tall,
Not suffering, but why?

Perhaps a trial had ended,
He seemed relaxed and pleased
To be a dancer summoned,
Not cast upon his knees

❖ ❖ ❖

UNLIKE YOUR OWN

When I think of love I have not given
How by the love of Christ can I be shriven?
Time will not repeat nor can that grace
Of love for love be now by love retraced

Over, done with, never to return
The loved one's need for love that I have spurned,
Is this not damnation to the soul,
A never-ending hurt, a creature's dole

O Lord accept this pleading of distress
Hopeless as it is, be merciful and bless
This hopelessness

This is my Babylon where I sit down
Here is my harp of sorrow, piercing crown,
My cross unlike Your own

❖ ❖ ❖

I HAD FORGOTTEN…

I had forgotten that he is an orphan
And so while outside seeming whole
He cracked in crazy pieces deep within,
The sanctuary darkness of the soul

It cleft, the inner heart was broken
And now the real one is the damaged one,
The false one beats in front,
No chambered pump, a bloodless shunt

If all were plain, uncovered what we are
There would be endless weeping were we bare,
There would be risen welted scars
That would be common, anyone's affair

❖ ❖ ❖

MORE FRIGHT THAN HE HAD EVER KNOWN

A young man pushed a baby stroller,
On his shirt I saw embossed
Hail Satan, as if damned forever,
His god a demon of the lost

One I know confided this:
He does not hell's allegiance own
For if he did he would confess
More fright than he had ever known

In battle Light and darkness meet,
Renegades have much to dread,
But there will be such grim retreats
And may the Light forgive the dead

❧ ❧ ❧

Pavel Chichikov

THEY COME WITH WINE

Perhaps it's time to board the Ark?
The rain is not so heavy, long,
It falls twelve hours through the dark,
But demon clouds have not prolonged
That darkness into day, nor raised
The floods of waters or the tides

Noah, what to take aboard
In case the storm arrives?
Only what I can afford
My children and my wives,
My property and such that I
Esteem the apple of my eye

Noah, look ahead, up high,
The tempest is about to break
About your snowy head, so why
Not go aboard, for pity's sake?
What storm, what clouds, what rain?
When all is done I will remain

Noah, stand, the tempest comes,
Lead the creatures up the plank,
The winds arrive, the downpours drum,
The clouds expel the seas they drank
Let me sleep, I still have time
And here my children come with wine

❖ ❖ ❖

OLÉ

The sun danced Fandango
With the tall tree's shadow,
A shy one with a crest
Played the hollow castanet

One arm of the wind
Bowed the branches' violin,
But O the bright guitar
Of that strident yellow star

❖ ❖ ❖

PYTHON

The snake began to squeeze our chests so long ago
That history had just begun, the state to grow,
Uruk of the pyramid, Memphis the White Wall
Sparta, Athens, Macedon, Rome before the fall

Mongolia and China, Imperial Japan
A python more than ten feet long is stronger than a man,
The serpent squeezes harder, the lungs begin to fail
The larger is imperium, the python grows in scale

Germany and Russia, Stalin in his prime
Around the ribs of nations the snake begins to climb,
But now it is so powerful there is no place to hide
For such a great constrictor can squeeze from the inside

❖ ❖ ❖

YOU TORE A PAGE...

You tore a page from Job to roll a cigarette
And as you tore the flesh of God from Him
So from your dying body will be torn your limb

You bragged of how you burned away
The flesh of God from the body of His name
So will those who take your limb show off the same

But still if you profess your shame and plead
For rescue and forgiveness in the dark and pain
Christ will come in mercy, love, and you will live again

❖ ❖ ❖

BECAUSE YOU CALLED

Ever since damned August of 1945
Shock waves have been rolling
Towards us through the decades

The fables of the human race
Instruct us in an endless final resolution
But waves move forward through the crippled centuries

A wave that never dampens
Clots of thunderous murder in the atmosphere,
A hemorrhage congealing in prophetic dreams

Although it comes with impulse and momentum
Though other lives were saved
It gathers up the future not yet born

Those who know it hear the syllables of thunder
In the sanctuary year,
Await this month and hour and the moment

Around us darkness, day and night
As were the days before the Resurrection
Although it seemed to others as the sun

The dead will seem again
To rise in praise and anguish from their graves
But only for a moment as the night rolls in

When the final storm appears we are appalled
To think we have deserved such desolation—
Master, I am here, it says, because you called

❀ ❀ ❀

1927

Revolution virgin-pure
Covered now in filthy sores,
I wonder what he'd think of this:
The paradox of class and war
Between the lowly and the state—
No servant of the Comintern
Foretold which class the Party ate:
I knew him at one hundred one

Channeled Chinese generals
For the International,
Tangled with the Kuomintang,
Came to grips with Capital
In California and Beijing—
Went to prison for a strike
And violent revolution's sake,
A kind of prophet-priest of Marx—
Of China now what would he make?

O morbid sour comedy—
Satirize such sacrifice,
Grip the bleak absurdity,
Who would place faith in Lenin twice?
Or secular Leviathan,
Idol in this life alone,
Butcher of the rights of Man
Sower of the seeds of stone,
And yet the faith was genuine:
The old man whom I met back then

❖ ❖ ❖

AN EVIL DREAM

Based on the Russian folk song "Oy, To Ne Vecher"

I had a dream, an evil dream
For as the night was falling I
Rode out upon the steppe, it seemed
As if the world itself would die

My horse, my crow-black horse began
To shiver underneath my grip,
And then in some dread fright he ran
Blood and foam around the bit

And then as if in swift attack
A fearful wind rose in the east,
My horse began to arch his back
And buck like some demented beast

The wind blew up into a gale
And snatched the cap from off my brow,
What fever dream this gruesome tale?
What prophecies do dreams allow?

Master, here's the sense I feel
The wind is death, the cap your head
Which you will lose to sharpened steel,
So that to you the world is dead

❈ ❈ ❈

IN WHICH THE DEAD ARE MET

I saw the man last night
Perspective new, resentment gone
We decided to be friends
He died ten years ago
But quarrels end

As Christ walked through a door
Though it was closed
So all go out again
Through rooms we have not seen before
We do not end

How can we forgive, forget?
Nothing is forgotten yet
It seems a trifling when
There is no end beyond the end
In which the dead are met

❖ ❖ ❖

Pavel Chichikov

A FORM OF LIGHT

Whose gleaming dust are you? said He,
Will you agree to a bargain?
I can arrange for you to be
A falcon or a salmon

You could command the bright updrafts
Of the mighty hills of heaven,
The souls of purgatory laugh
That will be there by evening

You might be flashing in the stream
That issues from My fountain,
Scales of gold and ruby gleam
Beneath My silver mountain

But I have thought another change
Could be the one to fit you,
A body that will seem most strange
Though it will not upset you

It is the glory of the joy
With which you are endowed,
This body I will not destroy
For it does not suit the proud

But you must be agreeable
To be clothed in such attire,
A form of light most beautiful
For angels to admire

❖ ❖ ❖

LOOK

They were surprised, dumbfounded when He held up the
    bread
Said: Look this is My body, on which you shall be fed,
And when he took the cup of blessing in His grip
And said this is the blood of Me, they felt their reason slip

But He had raised the dead ones, and driven demons out
From where they held the paralyzed—He made those
    devils shout:
You are the Son of God, have mercy on us all—
Even devils know the Lord, that He is their downfall

And when He fed five thousand they had partaken some
And when He cured the sightless, and vivified the dumb
And when He was transfigured to radiance of wonder
And when the heavens spoke to Him in syllables of thunder

They had no heart to doubt Him, and so they freely supped
The blood of their devotion, His life's blood in a cup,
For though it is forbidden by commandment of the law
It was a cup made lawful by astonishments they saw

And though it is forbidden to eat the flesh of Man
They had seen Him baptized in the Jordan as it ran,
And they had watched Him tread on the Sea of Galilee
And so they ate the flesh of Him, the same as you and me

❊ ❊ ❊

ELOQUENT OF LOVE

He's got a twist that makes his face go sideways,
Stumps a stick, his limp is from Vietnam,
Wounded grievously but now he stays
Inside the small-town refuge where he's from

Bennie stops for coffee at the shop
And asks them if his tab is still accepted,
Your credit's fine they say, the bill adds up,
But someone else at month's end often pays it

The local banker doles his money out
One day's worth of pension at a time,
Give him more he'd give away the lot,
A benefactor down to his last dime

His speech is slow and difficult but then
Eloquent of love our little Ben

❖ ❖ ❖

TWELVE GALLANT RIDERS

Twelve gallant riders came riding up the hill
All were in their costume of customary drill,
The first was tall and slender, white his face and eye
His breath he froze upon me as he came riding by,
The second was his equal, except that he was short
He seemed a brave outrider, the first one's bold escort,
The third was fierce of aspect, but with a secret hope
I read upon his countenance, he passed me at a lope,
The fourth one was a woman with flowers in her hair
That covered up the saddle, a drapery most fair,
The fifth another maiden her saddle cloth was green
She rode the finest chestnut that ever I have seen,
The rider next among them, the bridle in her hand
Cast a look around her at the flourish of the land,
And then a stately rider riding tall, erect
Upon a mighty stallion, the summer to inspect,
Another came behind him, full of flesh and blood
A very hardy rider, mature in his manhood,
Behind him though not tardy, a rider on a mare
Who seemed to look around him for a face that was
    not there,
The tenth one was a smaller horseman with a smile
His pony was a fat one, and yet could trot a while,
The second from the last horse, the mane of which was gray
Seemed ill-disposed to frolic but gravely made its way,
The last one had a litter cinched firm upon its side
A very modest pony but it cantered on with pride

❖ ❖ ❖

SURGEON

The man with one arm, sawed to the armpit
Walks to the garden, swinging a bucket,
Casts me a cautious glance to the side,
Smiles a shy pleasantry, we are allied

In our own mutilations, he of the war,
I see, look away from it, quick to ignore,
I from a multiple failure of love
A cut to the quick I can never remove

This morning the lightning commanded the eye
As if in my dreaming a flame cauterized
The wound of an evil that bleeds in a sleep
Where all of our lesions are draining and deep

So it will be when the surgeon arrives
Who can salvage the limbs that once were alive

❖ ❖ ❖

OU SONT LES VACHES D'ANTAN?

The bull seal must retire from the beach,
Inflated be the nose, the sultan dies,
Neck engorged the master is impeached
No matter how shot through with blood the eyes

That huge gross body, slack, will draw decay
Into a mass of jelly-blubber, skin;
Gulls sweep down to pull the meat away
From one another, scarf a specimen

A leading seal permits no bellow-fellows—
All the cows are mine that I can reach,
My rivals tusked and driven to the shallows—
A bull seal must retire from the beach

Where does my power go when it is dead?
It is conserved like energy until
The last bull seal to be alive is fed
To scavengers who snarfle up their fill

Where are the fearful, lumping off in fear?
Where are the timid cows of yesteryear?

❖ ❖ ❖

Pavel Chichikov

DAWN OF FLAMES

Waiting here is what we do, the time not ours
Nor is there any sign of dawn on this cold shore,
White sand freezing to the foot, the ocean rolls
Inward from profundity, deep and old

Along a ridge of sand there is a line of huts,
The kind of hovel tumbledown that tramps construct,
Soot black, coated with the grime of burning rubber,
Diesel oil, wet cardboard and some wood or other

There I see my boyhood friend, bone-chilled and huddled
Near the smoking wizened fire, smirched and troubled,
Bent in frozen poverty and dumb distress,
Camped above a wordless sea in wordlessness

Then I walk along the border of the surf,
The gentle speaking of the waves that break and cough
As if they come from distances of long ago,
Primeval waves that break unhurried, sure and low

Above, the sky begins to brighten to a band
Of rose, deep rose above the ocean and the land—
Bow down to the Emperor a voice proclaims
And I who hear it bow down to the dawn of flames

❋ ❋ ❋

TO MIMIC PROPHECY

Raining red hot metal
Re-entry of a missile
Into a dark blue sea

The ripping of the atmosphere
Guttural transforming roar
Of spending energy

I saw it fifty years ago
And three
Planted in my memory

Suppose those dreadful blossoms grow
Warheads tumble and then slow
Above a city's trees?

What then if the people heard
That ripping sound, a metal sword
Of robot arms and armories?

It would be parody fulfilled
Apocalypse of human skills
To mimic prophecy

Preposterous how we intend
To imitate what God may send
In our midget jealousy

As if we humans could forestall
Whatever ending might befall
Our human history

By working to anticipate
Completion of our mortal state
Our own finality

❖ ❖ ❖

A GIFT

Seven stars came dancing from far Aldebaran
Some have called them sisters, progenitors of man,
Asterisms merely, or the profile of the bull,
Perhaps a sail of sheepskin or the curling of the wool

But these are not the symbols of a fable or a myth,
They are no fabrication of the masters of untruth,
See how far they travel as they flee Aldebaran
A hundred forty years is the distance that they scanned

I saw them settle lightly in the tangle of a wood,
The hazel and the briar where the tulip poplar stood,
Outlined by a blackness against a cloth of lights—
The winter night was folding in a flashing of delights

They settled in the branches that quivered with caresses,
So happy were the sisters, so heavy were their tresses
A fall of light had covered the winter naked trees,
Translucent were the garments of the dancing Pleiades

Those who cannot see them have been enchanted blind,
Imprisoned in the fortress of the apprehended mind,
But those who have remembered what they have always
    known
Will bring a gift of dancing to the everlasting Throne

❖ ❖ ❖

ANDREW

Andrew is an old plow horse
With honey-golden hair,
Thick of leg and massive, coarse,
Repulsive to a mare

A rarity, exotic, odd,
Not many farms can use
A horse to slice and drop the sod,
Useless old Andrew

They kept him mostly in a field
A grazing ornament,
All his virtues were concealed,
The boss indifferent

A riding stable took him on
To be a placid steed,
A broad of back phenomenon
But worthy of his feed

If they let him take the reins
And walk as he would go,
He stops against a fence and turns
As if he plowed a row

❖ ❖ ❖

AND YET WITHIN

These messengers will come from far away
Unholy gifts and signs of power with them,
We will misinterpret their displays
But they will not have come from any heaven

They will show what has no explanation
By any art or science we have known,
They will use our cities as their mansions
The seas and heights forbidding as their thrones

Almost all will give their full allegiance
Except there will be some who have the wit
To feign obedience and dedication
And yet within these ones will not submit

These messengers a meaning will deliver
From powers greater than the ones they own,
And though they seem all-powerful and clever
They too owe allegiance to a throne

These messengers are not of flesh and blood
Although they can engender what they need,
They are the forces of no personhood
And if destroyed they will not, cannot bleed

And yet within there is a force unending
That will resist and overcome at last,
Although the power bidden is unbending
And by the measure of the dead is vast

❖ ❖ ❖

Pavel Chichikov

INSIDE

Within a chest with triple locks the secrets of the soul,
None but One can look within, examine or extol,
The first confines the yearning heart that loves or will not
    love,
The second lock holds in the light that death cannot remove,
The third restrains the joyful soul and endless unity
And only He who made the locks can also turn the key

❧ ❧ ❧

BIG BABY

How fragile, frail this bright blue bulb
And all who live upon it,
Oceans swaddle up the globe,
The ice cap for a bonnet

A baby with a baby's head
And brittle fontanel
That is the rifted ocean bed—
The baby breathes and swells

Just like an infant in its nap
It waves its legs and snores,
And so the restless oceans lap
Against the riddled shores

If this infant should awake
There will be some surprise
When all the seas and oceans shake
To see the baby rise

❖ ❖ ❖

TRUE LOVERS

When she sleeps beside you bless
The deepened breath and sigh,
She has traveled to the west
To where no one can die

The sun descends to find a day
Where none but she can follow,
Though travelers will seldom stay
But will return tomorrow

Beside and near, beside and near
The world that has no end,
Though to the soul it may appear
A citadel or friend

An angel or an animal
A journey or a wood,
Where trees are speaking sentinels,
A symbol understood

Each and all must go alone
Until they wake from slumber,
Two and two around the Throne
True lovers without number

❧ ❧ ❧

FIRE AND RUST

They don't even know that fire is hot.
　　　　　　—George Orwell, *Inside the Whale*

Do you know that the rabble rose up in Byzantium,
Rebels opposed to the rule of Justinian?
He was ready to flee to the fleet in the harbor
While the streets of Byzantium sweltered in murder

Then Theodora the bear keeper's daughter,
The Empress unyielding, disdaining the slaughter
Spat at his feet, at his slippers of gold—
"I'm more of a man and not a cuckold

"Run if you want to, I'm staying right here,
In guts and audacity more than your peer,
Run to the ships, I'll stay and repel
The revolt of these midgets and send them to hell"

The Emperor stiffened and said he would stay—
"Why should a wolf be afraid of his prey?
Call out the troops and lock up the gates
While the mob at the Hippodrome stupidly waits"

They locked up the Hippodrome, slaughtered the lot—
Now, in our century, all would be shot;
Believe at some moment in time there will be
A revolt in a Hippodrome similarly

There will be empresses urging their mates
To call out the troops and lock up the gates,
Fire is hot though some may not trust
That fire is quick and cleaner than rust

❖ ❖ ❖

RANSOM

At Cajamarca the Emperor
The captive king, Atahualpa
Told a cruel Conquistador
That he would fill his prison room
With gold and silver, his heirlooms
As high as he could reach by hand,
As high as emperors can stand

The Inca's ransom saved him not
He was strangled by garrote—
But where in all the world to find
A ransom right for all mankind,
What mass of treasure can we pay
For savagery, to heal away
Tortures, massacres and grief,
For which of these exists relief,
Sufficient hoard to compensate
Atrocities of war and state?
Whom to pay and in what hall
Could such redemption fit for all?
Even were the sky enclosed
What payment made for all of those?

If all the world were poured with blood
And acrobats on shoulders stood
To mark a line around the sky
Would one less human being die?
And yet a body's sacrifice
In blood and flesh—it did suffice

❊ ❊ ❊

ON THE RIDGE LINE

Empty of human affection
The soldiers prepare for war,
They care not for pity, discretion
Nor what they are fighting for

Trained from their birth to take orders,
They love to be up and away,
In combat they offer no quarter,
Killing for them is fair play

In the air they have eyes like tornadoes,
At sea they are swifter than winds,
Their hearts are afire and hollow
Their bodies elastic and finned

Their substance is general issue
With legs of the four and the six,
Metal and flesh is their tissue,
Bio-mechanical mixed

I see them ahead in the vastness
That lies between future and past,
But if you have hopes of remoteness
What figures are those? Need you ask?

❖ ❖ ❖

THE PEOPLE SHOUT

Darts to the bull behind his spreading horns,
Vexatious but not crippling and yet
With each new stinging dart he can't forget

Forward, forward at the cape of red
That swinging lure, that irritating cape
And to the side a stiffened, posing ape

Ignore the darts, the pain, it doesn't matter
To the strength of one who was a king
Of cows, of calves, who aren't in the ring

Forget the meadow, now there is the sun—
Heavy is the monstrous head, the Minotaur,
The flashing light, the all-surrounding roar

Temper is the killer and the darts
Which dangle from the hump behind the head,
The curtain shows him death, and it is red

So to every power comes another power—
Until the horses drag the bull away
The people shout: Olé!, Olé!, Olé!

❖ ❖ ❖

ALCIBIADES

Sumptuous amoral prince, the people's champion
Who could at once inspire them, and see them all undone,
Conspirator and maestro of effrontery, intrigue—
He undermined confederates with whom he was in league

Tongue of honey, tongue of oil, a biting tongue of scorn,
A purple-wearing democrat unto the manner born,
An admiral without a peer who could a fleet betray,
A conqueror of armies who might also slip away

Icy-hearted butcher but a fearless warrior,
Genius of victory and double-dealing cur,
Prodigal of promises of which a few he'd keep,
All at once an open face with motives fathoms deep

Virtuoso liar, fascinating wit,
Magnetic and appealing, a subtle hypocrite,
His enemies were mesmerized, his friends were all beguiled
Even when he strangled trust and left them all defiled

Will we ever see his like, who is so long remembered?
Athens flourished long ago, its power long dismembered,
Beware the talents of the one without a doubt or fear,
He will emerge when noon is high and shadows disappear

❖ ❖ ❖

Pavel Chichikov

AND WHAT IS THAT?

Some who follow football with their mortgaged eyes
Say the Bronze Age was the age of primitives,
An age of stupid warriors and brazen lies

What coming into daylight differs now?
Had they different dying, knew the less?
Who owns smaller ignorance—confess!

Thunder, smoke and wonder are the same
Descending on Mount Sinai or a dreadful city—
These are the blinding messages of darker secrecies

Children rising from the circle where they sat
Fly to where the joyful duty has begun
To praise the everlasting light—and what is That?

❖ ❖ ❖

FLOWER DEEP

Simple and harmonious, the bed is large, well-made
The room is unembellished, precise attention paid,
Some might call it luxury and Spartan opulence,
But no one here but me, a bit of loneliness

Another room adjoining, I hear the women speak,
Double doors to cross, their company to seek,
Hear the women talking, conversing of some thing,
Disregarding what I am, a breeze the doorway brings

Planning for a journey, both of them deceased,
Neither one anointed or shriven by a priest,
Not friendly when they were alive, but now good friends
    enough,
The rooms go on who knows how far, but not beyond belief

The rooms are where we started from when we awoke from
    sleep
And where the beds already made are buried flower deep

❧ ❧ ❧

FIFTY MEGATONS

Lopshenga is a settlement alongside the White Sea,
Tundra, sand and shingle, unreachability,
A dozen houses, kitchen gardens, potatoes and some greens,
But people live by fishing, according to their means

A radio for medical removal or advice,
Say a body breaks a hip by slipping on the ice,
A coffin for a burial is carried by flatbed,
There is no formal carriage for the isolated dead

I flew in once by helicopter one long summer day
Only for some hours before I went away,
That is how they liked it when the Oblast or Moscow
Stretched out an arm and finger to the people long ago

Excellent it is to be remote and out of reach
When government is well-disposed to sanction or to preach,
Hopeful were the villagers that Moscow could forget
Their minimal existence where the sea and tundra met

But over the horizon once, near Novaya Zemlya
A giant detonation made a frightening aurora,
The burst of an effusion rose of fifty megatons—
No matter how remote they were, they were the closest
    ones

❧ ❧ ❧

THE SECRET HOLY ONES

They had Russia for seventy years, and Russia is dying—
They say it was Stalin's fault, but he was the serpent
Who hatched from the serpent's egg of the Party

Yaroslav the Czech (strange name)
Organic chemist at the State Academy
Told us of the factory where thousands died from year to
    year

And I said: Russia is dying, and they looked astonished,
Looked astonished that someone had said it—
Those who have no God will have no progeny

Pascal said: Man secretes evil as the bees secrete honey,
And yet there are the secret heroes, unknown saints
And even holy ones unknowing of their holiness

When they came back from the camps
They looked like those whose dyings were postponed
Until some better time and bowls of kasha

I saw them on the Arbat, their crudely lettered signs,
As if some faded icons had descended from the pillars
To walk the streets of Moscow in the cold

For those who are tormented and yet do not torment
Become the secret holy ones of this indifferent world
As are the ones who secretly have love to spare

❖ ❖ ❖

Pavel Chichikov

THE LAKOTA DEACON

One of the first Lakota deacons
Told me in the old classroom
The others had gone to the spirit world—
Through the window we could see
The tawny grass of a cold prairie—
Into the spirit world out there?
If not to the broken lands, then where?

Not to the sweat house but the altar
They went then and traveled farther—
The dead Lakota deacons went
Into the world of the sacraments,
The brilliant world by us forsaken,
Concealed now but not mistaken—
They could not consecrate but raised the Light

Through the bitter night he slept
And dreamed of where the Host was kept,
He was the only one remaining
In this dark world the light sustaining

❖ ❖ ❖

HANSEL AND GRETEL

Wandering, wandering, Hansel and Gretel
Into a wildwood corrupted with evil,
Within there's a cottage alluring and sweet,
The witch of the famine preparing to eat
The flesh she can gather, the flesh she can snare:
"Come little children, brood of despair,
Hungry I am, forever will be
For I never will beg or put down the knee,
By force and by cunning, by will and by ways
Whoever I tempt here I keep and I slay"
Said the witch of the wildwood, recruited by darkness
That ageless old sorceress

So came the children, hungry and thin
To the cottage of evil, the evil within
And she thought from the barefooted sound of their trust
That someone could tempt them with cake or with crust,
With cream of the almond, both bitter and dry
That she mixed with the batter of promise and lie,
The brick and the mortar were bone meal and blood
As red as the sunrise that pours through the wood;
So jealous their stepmother, stubborn and cruel
That she hissed and denied them a taste of the gruel,
Persuaded their father to lead them astray
Then go away

Hansel and Gretel, what will you do now,
Can God in His mercy this evil allow?
"Nibble on this and nobble on that,"
Said the witch to the children, "to make you both fat—
Marzipan chimneys and shortbread for bricks,
Sugar-spun windows for peeking and licks—
Step over the threshold, come into my parlor

Pavel Chichikov

No need to look famished—no need for that pallor"
But when they stepped in she grabbed them and shook
Them both by their napes—"You surely mistook
My offer for charity, now you must work
And better not shirk"

"Gretel," she growled, grabbed by the neck:
"Here's a broom, there's the room, let me see not a speck"
Gretel would sweep and the creature would search
For the speck of a fly, an invisible smirch,
Then scatter the cinders and coals from the fire,
Crumble them freely with mud from the mire;
Hansel she thrust with a shove in a cage:
"You'll taste very fine with salt, pepper and sage—
Sausage I'll make from your entrails, my lad,
But first you'll be fattened, so don't look so sad"
She fed him with flesh that she kept in a jar—
He thrust out the bones through the bars

At last she grew fretful with slaver and greed,
The old cannibal dreamed of a roast for her feed,
So she ordered the girl to heat up the fire
While she paced with impatience and danced with desire—
"Not enough, not enough, not hot enough, lass
Heat it as high as makes sand into glass"
Then leaping with rage she said: "Leave the flames be
I'll show you how torrid, like this, look at me"
She opened the door to the oven and bent
But the girl pushed her forward and in it she went,
First went the body and then went the toes,
The door was slammed closed

Frightful the screaming, the sorceress cooked,
While Gretel fetched keys that had hung on a hook
And let go her brother, released from duress,
No longer the meal for the ogress-mess—

They listened in wonder as shouting returned
Though one would expect that the monster had burned:
"I burn and I burn but I can't be consumed,"
Said the witch from the fire, "and can't be exhumed,
Flame unforgiving, flame with a grip
That will not let go and will not let slip,
How long must I burn here before I am free
From what I am, me?"

Then as they watched, a shadow appeared
On the wall of the cottage, but not what they feared,
A glorious angel that stood there upright
A pattern of rainbows that dazzled the sight,
Said to the children: "Now I must try
To save the old creature who's trying to die,
I must find a good place on her ruinous soul
I can grip with the force that iniquity stole,
A place that can give of itself, not extract
What it never created, the love that it lacked—
Wait while I search what she thought, what she dreamed
While in pain the witch screams"

❖ ❖ ❖

GRAY GEESE

Gray geese flocking on a lawn,
Small heads, small brains, flight muscles slack
Until they rise to breast the dawn
Like full rigged vessels, wings drawn back

On waves of air instead of sea—
And have you seen them brace to land,
Balance on the air as we
Push away from death and stand

And if these tiny souls can take
Such fleets so bravely through the sky
Each following the other's wake,
What risings of us when we die?

Was it then a metaphor
Of all the dead uplifting when
The hosts of heaven go to war
And Christ calls up the souls of men?

What flight, what air, what boundless space
What great migration overhead
When by the rising of His face
Christ calls up the dead

❀ ❀ ❀

ANCIENT GOVERNMENTS

Above the monument to Grant
Ospreys in the winter trees
Scan the Mall for game to seize

Storms have driven them away
From brackish waters in the Bay—
Beneath the Capitol's west wall

They push their curving pinions wide
Duck their heads and launch
Into a silent glide

Below a broken caisson rolls,
Brazen gunners on parole
From metal immobility

Frantic horses on the run
Troopers shouting, sabers drawn
Charge the fire of the guns

Vigilant the frozen stare
Of Grant astride who faces west
Toward Lincoln in his marble chair

When ancient governments of men
No longer fill their rooms
War will end

Trees will stretch their limbs and grow
And from the north
Come wings of silent snow

❧ ❧ ❧

MODEL TRAINS

I saw them watching model trains
Run past the towns of long ago
On brisk and snug December nights,
Lighted windows, powdered snow

Illuminated cars that climbed
From track to track and bridge to bridge,
Passed like shuttles through and through
A fir-grown plastic mountain ridge

Trains that carried company
To bring some faithful Christmas Eve
While to and fro the long trains ran
As if a unity to weave

Saw with open-mouthed beguilement
Safe and spotless minor towns,
The many shops and private homes,
The drive-in-diners in the round

Saw them watch a model world
That came a time, will not come back,
Although the copied trains recur
Along an endless railroad track

They climb aboard those mini-trains,
Sightsee the past, but they pass through,
No longer stop where once some did
When young and round the world came new

I smell the scent of frost on fur
The coats the women wore, the light
That comes from dusk and happiness,
That seemed to be a promised night

❖ ❖ ❖

THE CREATURES PETITION GOD

This is too much our Lord, our God,
This burden that You weighed upon us,
Two-legged like the Ostrich, odd
Head, face and hands, viviparous

Today I saw one lead a horse
Around and round a ring by reins,
Weakly was the human boss,
Stonewall was the horse's name

We who live below the soil
Among the blades of grass, the leaves
See with horror their turmoil—
They rob and dig and burn, those thieves

We do the work, we shift the earth
We move the minerals and gases,
Death to life and life to death,
All that springs and all that passes

He's the favorite, the waster,
What's he for and why is he?
Not so clever ape-imposter,
No fur, no tail, can't swing from trees

Then the Lord looked down, looked in
Agreed the justice of their grumble,
You of wing and leg and fin,
He is My venture and My gamble

If he will not learn to cherish
Love and keep and praise you all
As mine, my own, then he will perish—
Wild again will be Stonewall

There is another place I keep
And there he may be taken in,
But first in sorrow he must weep
Who has no wing to fly, no fin

❖ ❖ ❖

Pavel Chichikov

TIGERS SURROUNDED THE HOUSE LAST NIGHT

Tigers surrounded the house last night,
Eyes of the yellow and teeth of the white
To guard and to question, to search and to find,
Moonlight and shadow, the flesh and the mind

Where is the cub of the winter snows?
The queen of the tigers wanted to know,
Prepared to be patient they stood or they prowled
While over the rooftops night like a cowl

Drew over the head of the sleeping town
While the moon to the westward sank and went down;
Where is the cub of the pure and the wise?
Ask the angels of God in their earthly disguise

The queen of the tigers has entered the room
Where the sleepers are sleeping but who will wake soon,
But she leaves when she's told to, biddable, wild,
By the window that's open, to look for the Child

❖ ❖ ❖

CALCULATORS

Rank on rank and row on row
They sat on high and watched the show,
Those privileged and lofty fans
Of knights in armor and life spans

Crows and ravens on the spot,
Connoisseurs of knightly rot;
But there are birds possessing thumbs
And counting-fingers who do sums

To add their profits in the wars
Which publicly they must deplore;
When the cleansing fire ends
They all descend and only then

To pledge sincerely their regret
For all the young who won't beget,
And think of ways to justify
The dead who never multiply

❖ ❖ ❖

COALS

What would I see if I became light?
The world would unfold around and recede,
Black at the sides the front would be bright
If I were a being who lived at light speed

Ahead there would be a bright shining circle
Where I could become the brightness of me,
Around and behind the dark of a tunnel,
How do we know what the buried can see?

We are the embers that flush into flame
When the breath of the Spirit blows down on the coal
Of that which is lifted, unburied, the name
That we give to the dark and inflammable soul

❖ ❖ ❖

THE BATTLEFIELD OF WRATH

Blind, blind, blind—dust thrown in our eyes,
Everything you love, it says, grieves for love and dies,
It warns against a seeing, it promises a sleep,
I will be your eyes it says, your suffering will keep

I saw a darkened battle, fighters on a plain
Who could not stop the fighting or heal the wounds of
    pain,
They struggled in a blindness for what the others sought,
Battle fever took them, sightless as they fought

Give us back our vision, we have the need to wake,
Darkness will be lifting, dawn about to break,
Battle comes on battle, they took our eyes away,
Plunge our eyes in water, see the light of day

Darkness was our vision and suddenly we see
The mountains that surround us of far eternity,
Now we leave our weapons and climb the winding path
That leads away from blindness, the battlefield of wrath

❖ ❖ ❖

Pavel Chichikov

A GLASS OF ORANGE JUICE

At a restaurant a man was seated
Eating by himself, his meal completed
I saw him lift a glass of orange juice
As from his solitude and loneliness
Hands with sudden tremulousness held
Transparency, a quivering compelled
By running waves of desolating power
Which shake and torment, scarify and scour—
Then were steady, then were soft once more,
Steadiness of hand, but not the core

What is in the deep of us which shakes
When memory of desolation breaks
On what we must remember when we think—
Who would not drown remorse, who would not drink?

❖ ❖ ❖

WAKES THE DEAD

War will come again
No one has abolished war
And you are fit for service

At home or in the field
In the city street
Or in the office

The sweet wine of the past
Gives heavy sleep and vivid dreams
But the bitter cup forthcoming
Wakes the very dead

❖ ❖ ❖

DARK LEGEND

I heard the sound of breaking glass
Shouting voices crashed against the windows,
A bank was darkened as the people passed

Then I heard more than a dozen
Gunshots, firing repeat,
From above I saw a squadron of policemen

Signaled by a gesture they,
Deafened by the sharp reports
Charged a silenced entranceway

Long ago, as if in some dark legend
Now forgotten, only I
Recall the violent circle closing in

Glass can always break, the captive treasure
Wait by night and day to be released—
It will submit to any seizure

By the serpent's honey-golden apples charmed
Adam would have worn a bandolier
If Adam had been armed

❖ ❖ ❖

PERMISSION

The paper which I carried said that I
Was qualified to board the plane and fly,
But at the boarding station what I heard,
Was: Monsieur would request of you a word

I tell you frankly, said and laughed Monsieur,
I really don't know what you're doing here,
You have not been so authorized to go
Aboard, you must for now remain below

Though before I thought I had prepared
Permission through a sorrow seldom shared,
It seems that I must wait for now until
I have been called, departure at His will

O Lord my God, my Savior sweet and kind,
You know each sway and movement of the mind,
But I not knowing yours must patient stay,
You will not let me early go my way

❖ ❖ ❖

THAT WELL

When I was a child of four
Beneath the surgeon's blazing light
I walked along a burning road
Sun upon me while I bled

By the road I saw a pump,
A handle to bring water up,
Iron black in summer heat,
I struggled near on my small feet

Oh pump of iron, pump of grace
I thirst while blood runs down my face,
Let me drink from that deep well
Of which the Christ of water tells

Foretelling then and now and when
Most merciful for us He sends,
As like a child I might attain
That well and ease my thirst again

❖ ❖ ❖

ANOTHER ADORATION

Master of the universe, said those three kings,
Unto your crèche in Bethlehem we bring these things:
A silver salver filled with many coins of gold
For which the brawny limbs of many slaves were sold;
Here a platinum tabernacle filled with myrrh
Stolen from some merchants by a murderer;
There a dish of diamond filled with frankincense
For which the Queen of Sheba had no recompense

While the infant Jesus shone like April sun
Around the crèche of Bethlehem there had begun
A murmuring from notables who had come by:
The luster of the tabernacle caught the eye,
Coinage weighed in estimation filled the mind
With guesses at the carets of it if refined,
The dish of hollow diamond tipped and emptied out
Beggared all the incense in it, have no doubt

Were these kings who visited the lovely Child?
Who but God Himself by gold is not defiled?

❖ ❖ ❖

EZEKIEL'S VISION

The creatures of the vision of the wheels
Adamant and powerful and real
Turned not but to go they would proceed
At some immeasurable, unhurried speed

Then there were the eyes within the round
Rims that rose and fell above the ground,
Amber was the radiance they shed,
Woke the life within the living dead

Loath to live they would not rise until
The force of fire overcame their will—
Up to me, you stubborn bones of man,
Reunite your flesh and bone and stand

Willful were the very bones: We dream
And all the desert round us only seems,
Still the Throne of fire dipped and soared:
Get up you dead alive! The daylight roared.

❖ ❖ ❖

DRAGON

An angled turn, the ancient Square
Close by Our Lady of Kazan,
The red brick of the old Museum,
The beast of half a megaton,
A mobile rocket, Topol–M

What would the ancient prophets say
Who once condemned Jerusalem
If they could see the sixteen wheels,
The cab, the launcher, the war head?

Ezekiel saw not so many
Wheels, nor suffered worldly dread—
It darkened daylight, rolled, eclipsed
The Kremlin's victory parade,
The creature of apocalypse—

This is the dragon we have made,
It would not swivel left or right
Nor rise as yet into the air,
This dragon rolling through Red Square

❖ ❖ ❖

F-16s

I heard the roar of F-16s
Cross the city overhead,
Sentries high on kerosene
Who on their airy pickets sped

And we beneath a city wall
Without a stone or battlement
Thought no more of our downfall
That such patrolling should prevent

But when the walls go up it means
There is a gate that must be closed,
Documents that must be seen,
Private life to be disclosed

So that at last the guards deform
The shape of life they should defend,
And no one knows of what they warn
Or if the siege will ever end

❖ ❖ ❖

LUKE 6:1–5

As the Lord's disciples
Walked the wheat field
Crushing the grain
To feed their hunger

As the farmer in Kansas
Tasted his sorghum
Crushing the grain
And savoring sweetness

So the Lord will crush the harvest grain
Lord of the Sabbath
Man of our sorrows
Before He tastes the world's ripeness

Harvest of spirits, harvest of souls
Sweetness of love
Or bitter with sorrows
Or bitter with madness

❧ ❧ ❧

A FACE WITHOUT A NAME

100 horses
1000 cattle
Ten thousand sheep

How many are enough
To propitiate the gods?

These idols are like us
Hungry, greedy, famished

These are gods we trust
And they are pitiless

Ten thousand sheep aflame
The wool gives off rank smoke

The horses were so beautiful
We fed them human flesh

The cattle had great horns
Like altars to be sacrificed

Burn them, burn them all
These idols will have more

We have sacrificed our sons
Because they told us to

God by god by god
They never let us go

That one has a name
And a face without a name

❖ ❖ ❖

Pavel Chichikov

ANCIENT ONES

Blue and green their globes of eyes,
The hunting of the dragonflies,
Hulls of crystal swivel, catch
The swarms arising from a hatch

Summon now the ancient ones,
The falcons of the Permian,
Great with rowing their wingspread,
They loop and stitch the sun with thread

But now in falls of yellow light
The little hunters turn in flight
To gaze with facets at the sun—
Summon now the ancient ones

❖ ❖ ❖

THE DINOSAUR ENCYCLOPEDIA

It makes me calm to see such stupid beasts
Who once alive, abundant in vitality,
Had brains that chickens easily exceed
And yet could flourish tranquilly and breed

Calming to behold the giant forms,
Instinctive reptile brains that drove the limbs,
The appetites with intellects so dim,
But flatulence as loud as thunderstorms

Magnificent and colorful, not proud,
Voracious but not criminal or cruel,
With every necessary grace endowed
But not the sense to ever play the fool

How restful must have been that era past
That now in mud solidified is cast

❖ ❖ ❖

Pavel Chichikov

IF CHRIST ROSE FROM THE TOMB

He thinks he may have known me, but I see
The uniform of 1943;
Dead in all but memory, alive,
He stares at me, my uncle has arrived

How strange it is to meet the dead and yet
There is no fearful sorrow or regret,
Puzzlement and slowly formed surprise—
What is death if no one ever dies?

Young as once and toughened and robust,
Dead and yet alive, composed and flushed,
Do we stand beyond the bounds of doom?
Who is dead if Christ rose from the tomb?

❖ ❖ ❖

THE RIVER OF EGYPT

They build a dam of sandstone blocks—
Manganese washed from the rocks
Turns the run a bloody brown
So that the snakes and minnows drown

Ferns, the pool where minnows swim
A summer refuge cool and dim
Red and sterile now until
The engineers have flushed the fill

But if the stream were flushed with blood
As human rage is wont to do
Who will remove the stain, or could?
Who will the damaged world renew?

❖ ❖ ❖

TO BE OF STARLIGHT
For BL

I did not recognize her, she had changed
Although the difference in her was not strange,
She has been gone for years and had returned
From where the ruins of the ego burn

Non ego sum and yet I am alive,
Burn it, burn the me that has a me,
Intrinsic, let the light in me survive
Shine like starlight through an apple tree

Let me shine like all the other lights
Around, above the crown and through the leaves—
I saw her in a dream the other night
Clean and new as God's unfallen Eve

And yet I knew her, how I do not know,
Something of the old within her showed,
But clear of skin and eye she came my way
To be of starlight on this holiday

❖ ❖ ❖

THE OLD MEN COME APART

Senility a spreading stain
The old men come apart like cardboard
Fall to pieces in the rain,

Quarrel, shout, their faces glum,
Bodies having been rebuilt
By knee and hip and their eardrums,

Whose fault is it that what was new
Becomes ramshackle, bent and frail,
Pleasure in it knocked askew?

Resemblance to the childish face
Visible inside the mask
That someone with a pen could trace

Where is that which might recover
All the pleasure in the world
To make them see and live it over?

Cardboard in a winter rain
The dying in them must dissolve
Until the child within remains

❖ ❖ ❖

COME WITH ME

Come with me to where the Milk House Ford
Is paved with cobbles, now so long ignored,
But once the wagons crossed and climbed a grade
To Seventh Street, a country road in shade

Blue-white milk that rocked inside the cans
Carried up to where a Safeway stands,
But then a store with yellow wheels of cheese,
Cracker barrels, apples, bins of peas

No so long ago, a hundred years
A little more, another hundred nears
When we will be forgotten as were they:
A century is counted day by day

Those who drove the wagons, dipped the milk
Have faded like a water mark on silk,
And those who stopped to watch the wagons cross
Are long forgotten, like the wagons lost

As shadows are forgotten as they slide
Along the ground although they never died,
So images of those who lived I see
Not faded, living, standing next to me

There's the wagon rattling, and the reins
Held loosely in the hand, the sound remains,
The shallows of the creek, the cobbles wet,
The images of old, I see them yet

❖ ❖ ❖

LEAVE IT BEHIND

I saw the cells of purgatory
When I was a child,
The menaces of royalty
In stiff brocaded gold

Stiff with unforgiving pain
They moved out from their cells
Where prisoners of hate remain
Inside their narrow hells

Underground along an aisle
They reached out for a touch,
A neediness which might defile,
Defilement in their clutch

Not till now to think that they
Had reached for artlessness,
Not on innocence to prey
But to be ill the less

Massive were the robes of them
Well stiffened with brocade,
Resentment sewn to every seam,
A nightmare they had made

But I passed on along the way
Between the kings and queens
Of unforgiving savagery
To tell what I had seen

❖ ❖ ❖

BREAD OF ICE

Do I not bleed money?
Are not my five wounds five decimal points?
Is not my crown a woven star of diamond?
Am I not scourged with your defaults?

Do I not bear a heavy cross of gold?
Does not my cup run over with petroleum?
Is not the spirit I breathe out the gas
Of the desert tombs?

This is my money*
Which will not be given up for you;
This is my blood
Which is too crystalline to flow

At the table of my sacrifice
The bread, which melts before you eat, is baked of ice

❖ ❖ ❖

---

*A phrase from *Chronicles of Wasted Time,* by Malcolm
Muggeridge

THE FISHERMAN'S WIFE

After the Brothers Grimm

A fisherman, the rolling seas,
The ocean leaps, a spanking breeze,
He's come with net and scaling knife
With orders from his old alewife
To hook or net a mighty school,
"Or don't come back," she says, "old fool."

So out he sails at her command
Until he's out of sight of land,
Stops and lowers down his net
(The wind is fierce, his slicker wet)
And still the savage wind increases
His little sail is slashed to pieces

Now the boat is knocked about,
The rollers march, the tempest shouts
When suddenly the windstorm dies—
"Have mercy on my soul," he cries
For now he sees a mighty fish
Too great to fit in any dish

Standing up between the swells
A halibut, he knows that well
But larger than he's ever known
And here he is at sea, alone—
"Have mercy," cries the fisherman,
"For here I am, ten miles from land."

He grips a gaff, for good or ill,
Hooks the fish beneath its gills,
Hauling now with might and main,

Pavel Chichikov

His muscles cracking in the strain
Until the fish is hauled aboard
"Give praise," he says, "and thank the Lord."

Holds his knife, about to gut
This huge and golden halibut—
"Be calm," it says, "and have no fear"
Uncanny is the voice he hears
As if a cold and brazen bell
Had rung a lingo from the swell

"Spare my life," exclaims the fish,
"And I will grant you any wish,
Be it gold, or be it fame—
Halibut the King my name."
The fisherman puts down his knife
Thinking of his greedy wife

Now the fisherman must think:
"Gold, or land, or food and drink?
I know what my wife might need—
Herring garnished with sea weed."
The fish can read his mind, declares:
"Go home, the herring will be there."

He sails for home and soon arrives.
The wife awaits with forks and knives,
Salt and pepper, olive oil,
The kettle standing on the boil,
Her clogs are tapping on the floor
As he comes bustling through the door

"What's this herring doing here?"
She yells at him. "It just appeared."
And he explains, "It came to be

Because a fish who rules the sea
Can give us anything we crave
From land or sea or sky or wave."

"And you chose herring, did you then?"
The woman shouts. "Why not the hen
Who lays a golden egg a day?
When God gave brains, were you away?
Go back and ask for something good
You good for nothing block of wood."

So back he goes where he before
Had met the fish—the sea waves roar—
Through the sails the tempest cuts,
He sees the golden halibut.
"Now," the king of oceans asks,
"Have you any little tasks

"To ask of me?" The man replies,
Shame in voice and cast of eyes,
"My wife's not satisfied, your honor
She's got an awful yen upon her
For gold and land and fine array
That she must have this very day."

"Go back again," replies the King
"Her wishes to your wife to bring,
Although her luck she may not like."
With fin and tail the waves he strikes
So that they boil up to the sky
And throw the little boat awry

Grim the heavy overcast
But still he reaches shore at last
Leaves the beach and jogs uphill

But stops, his mouth agape, stands still
Beholds a mansion where there'd been
A humble shanty to live in

Gardens, lawns, and topiary,
Tennis courts and statuary,
Many windows, doors, and wings
And other sumptuary things,
While at the doorway stands his spouse,
The titleholder of this house

"Not so fast," she tells her mate,
"Take off those dirty boots and wait
Until the butler brings your slippers,
And please strip off that awful slicker,
Don't drip water on the floor
Unless you'd like to get what for."

On and on she scolds and squalls
Until she drives him up the wall
As patient as he is by habit
(A husband meek as any rabbit)
Then, before he's had his meal
She tells him how she really feels

"The house and staff and lands are good,
But how to clinch our livelihood?
Investments, cash, and gilt-edged bonds
Of which the very rich are fond
Are what we need, and even more
Position to get in the door

"Of where the power truly lies,
Authority of ample size—
Tell the King of Fish I want

A bank that's amply stocked with quants,
A Senate seat with influence,
Make it senior—get you hence!"

Not even having drunk his soup
Her husband climbs aboard his sloop
And casts away—but now the sky
Is deadly gray, the storm clouds fly,
The sea a sickly, turbid black
On which he makes a foaming track

Up there rises on his lee
The halibut who rules the sea
Fixes him with steady gaze
And all his power he displays
By slapping up a mighty roar
Of waves that run from there to shore

"Now?" the creature wants to know,
As hurricanes of anger blow;
"Forgive me, sir, the urgency,
But this is what she wants of me—
A Senate seat, a bank, and then
Quantities of clever men."

"The stupid woman has her choice,"
It grumbles in a hollow voice
"Because you spared my life I give
These other wishes—go and live."
As quickly as the skipper can
He turns the boat and runs for land

The captain finds when he gets home
A capitol with shining dome
Marble steps, a portico

Pavel Chichikov

Where notables go to and fro
And there among them is his wife,
Satisfied? Not on your life

She grips him by the broad lapel
And groans, "I burn in living hell
Because I'm only one of many
But of respect there isn't any,
One monkey in a monkey troop
You salt seafaring nincompoop

"Go back again, you gollywog
And be it devil or Magog
You make that fish stand on its tail
And send me power without fail—
I want to be the President
And don't come back unless it's sent."

So off he goes once more—the waves
Beneath a storm both fierce and grave
Enough to sink a mighty ship,
Above the waves his schooner skips
The wind is like a pressing wall
And no evading it at all

The fish impending overhead
Now fills the fisherman with dread
And casts a baleful icy glance
As if to dare him to advance:
"The President she wants to be
I hope, good Fish, you won't blame me."

It only waves a mighty fin
As if its temper might wear thin,
The skipper cringes, turns away

Back to shore without delay
And up the hill to find his spouse
Oathed, installed in a White House

Behind her desk she thumps her fist
"I will have more, my grace insists
A greater place I do prefer—
This strength is only secular
You ancient salt-encrusted dope:
Tell the fish I would be Pope."

He cringes, shrugs his shoulders then
He turns around to sea again
Hauls the boat into a wind
Against the rudder almost pinned
By sweeping, biting angry gales,
He finds the fish and his heart fails

The halibut without a flip
Appears into a trance to slip,
It waves the fisherman away
Who cringes back without delay
To find ashore a mighty dome
Much higher than the one at Rome

He's blown inside by mighty winds
To see a gorgeous baldachin
An altar and a golden throne,
His wife upon it, proud, alone,
She gives to him a ring to kiss:
"I've never felt such joy as this

"For now I hold authority
Above the world, none are as me,
All must kiss my ring and kneel

And who from me such bliss can steal?
I have control of the divine
And all the rest of you are swine

"Why stay here when I can seize
Supremacy and be at ease,
Not president or emperor,
Why stick at lesser sway, what for?
Better still an iron rod,
A planet maker—why not God?

"I will give life and I will kill,
Let every creature do my will,
Go back and give the fish my charge
For I am great though he is large,
Though he is vast, I am the vaster,
God for me or world disaster"

Away the fearful skipper sails
The waves immense, the north wind wails
O halibut, O fish, O fate
What retribution must await?
But then a tiny voice, a squeak,
He hears the fish begin to speak

"No matter, do not fear, my friend
For every folly has an end
Return, a gift of peace is sent
The storm of madness will relent
For all begins where it began
The tree of Life and Death still stands."

And where the earthly powers walked
Upon the hill where power stalked
He finds the woman in the hut

She knew before the halibut
And herring boiling in a pot
And she contented with her lot

And as he watches from the beach
The waves of ocean in their reach
It seems to him that he is, too,
Contented with the mighty view
Although he knows, as dinner warms,
The sea is great with greater storms

❖ ❖ ❖

THE WEIGHT

The land
Because of our cruelty
Because of the martyrs of insolence
Because of the children tortured, abused
Because of the old ones abandoned, exposed
Because of the massacres, dreadful slaughters
Because of indifference to love and faith

Will be wiped away clean
Will be cleansed and scoured
We are all as one and none are divided

Only the martyrs of God can save
By the offering up of their agonies
Given for us in the mercy of Christ

For I saw how the ripples of evil spread out
From older to younger, to sons and daughters
Greater to lesser to child in the womb

Only the crucified God alone
Can bear up the weight of the suffering world
And carry it bleeding, cross and man

❖ ❖ ❖

LIGHT UNCONQUERED

In hac urbe lux solemnis
—Peter Abelard

Angels see as they look down
Azure oceans, wrinkled lands,
Silent planet, blue and brown,
In their silence mountains stand

Oceans spin invisibly,
Southern winds and silent wheat,
What of mankind can they see?
Rage, corruption and deceit

Still in this metropolis
Light unconquered, solemn peace,
In hac urbe lux solemnis
So will every shadow cease

❖ ❖ ❖

www.ingramcontent.com/pod-product-compliance
Lightning Source LLC
Chambersburg PA
CBHW022307060426
42446CB00007BA/736